OTHER NATIONS
An Animal Journal

Poems by
Maria Famà

PEARLSONG PRESS
NASHVILLE, TN

Pearlsong Press
P.O. Box 58065 | Nashville, TN 37205
http://www.pearlsong.com | http://www.pearlsongpress.com

Original trade paperback ISBN 978-1-59719-087-9
Ebook ISBN 978-1-59719-088-6

OTHER BOOKS BY MARIA FAMÀ

Mystics in the Family (2013, Bordighera Press, NY)
Looking for Cover (2007, Bordighera Press, NY)
Identification (2nd edition, Allora Press, Philadelphia, PA)
Italian Notebook (co-authored with Mary Russo Demetrick,
1995, Hale Mary Press, Syracuse, NY)
Identification (1991, Malafemmina Press, San Francisco, CA)
Currents (1988, Adams Press, Chicago, IL)

Library of Congress Cataloging-in-Publication Data

Names: Famà, Maria, author.
Title: Other nations, an animal journal : poems / by Maria Famà.
Description: Nashville, TN : Pearlsong Press, 2017.
Identifiers: LCCN 2017021238 (print) | LCCN 2017021318
(ebook) | ISBN
   9781597190886 (ebook) | ISBN 9781597190879 (trade pbk. :
alk. paper) | ISBN
   9781597190886 (ebook)
Subjects: LCSH: Animals—Poetry.
Classification: LCC PS3556.A4875 (ebook) | LCC PS3556.
A4875 A6 2017 (print) |
   DDC 811/.54—dc23
LC record available at https://lccn.loc.gov/2017021238

"We need a wiser and more mystical concept
of animals…They are not brethren,
they are not underlings; they are other nations,
caught with ourselves in the net of life and time,
fellow prisoners of the splendour and travail
of the earth."

HENRY BESTON
writer-naturalist
The Outermost House

This book is dedicated to the memory of my parents
and grandparents, who fostered a love of animals,
and to the memory of Skeeter,
my long-time feline companion.

Contents

Canyon de Chelly

A woman prays at Canyon de Chelly
the sun rises over
Spider Grandmother's sandstone spire.

    distant starshine
    warm first light
    sacred rocks, juniper trees, sage brush
    the wind is a presence
    one eagle flies overhead

spirit guides, come
animal mentors, come
a woman prays at Canyon de Chelly

    seashells of past ocean
    dry sands of the wash
    change and stay
    ancient Anasazi cliff dwellings
    present Navajo hogans
    change and stay

    hawk and owl
    sheep and herders
    cornfield and stream
    trees and scrub
    prairie dog and mouse
    change and stay
    sing the power of the pulse
    the holiness of sunshine on stone.

a woman prays at Canyon de Chelly
changes   changes
and stays.

LITANY OF MY PETS

From celestial waters and endless skies
From excellent sun, flowers, and grass
From perfect mooned nights and freshest of days
    take time

From your milk-boned, catnipped, toy-filled heaven
look down and remember me
    your devoted human

PRINCE, stately black and white lithe feline, who
at the sound of my stroller's wheels ran long-limbed
to meet my mother and me
    PRAY FOR ME

TICO, cheerful canary singer of intricate tunes, who
uncaged sat like a bit of morning sunshine on heads
and shoulders and never flew away
    PRAY FOR ME.

MUFFIN, tiger kitten martyr, who suffered a slow
painful death at the hands of "Old Man Hitler" the
poisoner of neighborhood cats
    PRAY FOR ME

ROAMER, red-necked Louisiana turtle, who arrived
tiny and scratching in a box through the mail and
grew strong and large enough to roam and catch
Philadelphia flies
    PRAY FOR ME

LUCKY, tawny part-hound puppy with bouncing nerves, who hid our winter caps in your dog house and ate my brother's jacket
PRAY FOR ME

CHICO, brave, turquoise parakeet survivor of a cat's claw, who never spoke but learned to wolf whistle and perch on my finger
PRAY FOR ME

WATCHFISH, golden, four-inch overeater, who watched and swam and swam and watched through the clear glass bowl of your small world
PRAY FOR ME

MIDNIGHT, ebony, green-eyed pussycat confidante, who was lost for one whole month and found your way home to me when I was eleven and grieving for you while recovering from an eye operation
PRAY FOR ME

FLIP, clairvoyant, majestic tabby ruler of home and alley, who climbed an electric pole and sent me a dream message to rescue you
PRAY FOR ME

SKEETER, my feline companion for twenty-one years, operatic, beatific, and beautiful pussycat, who rescued and comforted me each day
PRAY FOR ME

All my dears, sainted pets,
intercede for your human friend,
who loves and praises you still,
that she may share with you eternal joy.

AMEN.

Walpi, First Mesa

On the Hopi reservation
one cat, one dog followed me everywhere
waiting outside when I entered a home
I fed them each day at dawn and asked for guidance
"They are spirit friends," I was told.

Horses

Horses
    hats on their heads
    bows on their tails
    bags below their rump

sweat and pull
tourist packed carts
through hot   city   streets
    slow steps   and   pull
    slow steps   and   turn
    bus fumes
    car exhaust
    every day the load
    waiting for a break in the shade
    some oats   an apple
    till home   and   sleep

I sweat   and   look   for   a   job
on hot city streets
    slow steps   I turn a corner
    slow steps   I interview with a man
    who wants to know
    if I'll be a good horse
    wear a suit
    carry the workload
    from nine to five
    plus overtime

Horses
　　the man says
　　I   must   work   hard
　　pull   my   weight

Horses
　　I   dread   the   harness
　　fear the bit

Horses on asphalt
dreaming of meadows,
teach me patience.

The Lion

I await my trainer
She will come with a whip
She will come with a gun
I await my trainer
I shall dance through hoops of fire

When she comes I stand back
I roar, "This isn't me!"
My trainer doesn't care
She's here to do a job
The circus pays her and
I am an insignificant lion
I am here to do my job, my tricks.
My trainer gives me food
  if I am docile
  if I learn the cues
  if I wave my paws just so
My trainer says, "That's right, do it again"
I hear the whip
I roar
I hate the sound of the gun
I want to pounce on my trainer
  tear open her neck
  fling her away from me
  let her lay broken and bleeding
  in the corner of my cage
I will roar, "I am leaving!"

There are bars everywhere
No one is here from my pride
I am an insignificant lion
I await my trainer
She will come with a whip
She will come with a gun.

The Dolphin

I live alone in a Florida pool
I have a yellow plastic alligator for company.
It floats but cannot chirp nor click
It does not whistle nor form words
It cannot cuddle, it does not breathe
Yet I hold its tether in my mouth as
I swim round and round the pool
with it at my side

My yellow plastic alligator is hard
not soft and smooth as I remember
my mother, my siblings, and my playmates
Yet I pretend the yellow plastic alligator
  is my companion
I pretend it is my partner and my love
I swim round and round this blue pool
  and try to remember the ocean's taste

On Sundays I perform for humans
They clap and I pretend to laugh
My master gives me a fish for my dance

I live alone in a Florida pool
I think if I stay on the bottom long enough
I can pass to freedom
My yellow plastic alligator will not miss me.

The Parrot

My name is Monterey
I am green, blue, and yellow
My human is Gracie
She calls me Monterey
Beautiful Monterey. Monterey Beautiful

I live inside walls and perch in my wire and wood
Gracie gives me water and food
From the glass wall I see others
not as beautiful as Monterey
those who are not human who fly

I can fly a little
out of my wire and wood I fly and walk
Gracie tells me I am beautiful
Beautiful Monterey. Monterey Beautiful.

I didn't know the words
for the flames, the heat, the smoke
Gracie went out from the walls
I was alone
I saw an orange tongue leap up a kitchen curtain,
a fierce smell a gray cloud   danger
Monterey scared. Scared Monterey.

I squawked, coughed a bark, meowed
I cried like a baby human
and I sang

Yo ho ho and a bottle of rum
Row, row, row your boat
My wire and wood is in the parlor
The kitchen was red, black, and yellow

I sang
Sixteen men on a dead man's chest
to be brave
A gray cloud in the dining room
I coughed choked preened my green feathers
I called in my loudest voice
Monterey help. Help Monterey.

Row. Row. Help. Meow. Beautiful. Monterey. Help.
Yo Ho Ho and a bottle Monterey Help
Humans were outside the glass
They yelled and smashed the glass wall

My wire and wood and me were carried out
I say Hello   Hello
outside the walls
coolness and lots of humans
and those that fly perched up on swinging wires

Gracie has water in her eyes
I say Hello Mommy Gracie Hello
Monterey help. Help Beautiful Monterey.

NELLE

A small brown and white terrier, Nelle,
straight from France
lived next door to me for four years
with her French doctors
postdoctoral fellows at Jefferson Hospital

Nelle, in elegant collars and tasteful sweaters
paraded with her doctors proudly up Sigel Street
as if it were a Paris boulevard

For half a year
I chatted in English with the doctors
I greeted Nelle
"Hello, Nelle, how are you?"
Every day, Nelle stiffened, glared, growled at me

Then, one morning, as Nelle emerged
with her doctors for a walk
I said, "Hello, Yannick! Hello, Hèrvey!"
I looked at Nelle and said
"Bonjour, Nelle! Comment allez vous?"
Nelle wagged her tail, licked my hand,
I swear she gave me a smile

From then on
every day in my shaky French
"Bonjour, Nelle! Comment ça va?"
"Bonjour!" "Bonsoir!" "À bientôt, Nelle!"

Every day, Nelle bestowed
a precious lick of my hand, a welcome wag of her tail,
even a smile
Every day a little bit of French
for a thoroughly French dog
"Nelle, sa va bien?"
Every day for Nelle
"Bonjour!" "Bonsoir!" "Bonne Nuit!"
Until she returned to France
with her doctors.

"Adieu, Nelle!"
"Au revoir, Nelle, au revoir!"

JACK

In late 1929 right before my grandfather
left Sicilia again for *L'America*
he bought his children a puppy
to remember him by
gave the pup an American name, Jack

My father, Saruzzu, a boy of six, was entranced
my grandmother, twenty-nine and pregnant, was
worried
how could she feed a dog when
they hardly had enough to eat themselves
what if Jack ate their chickens
what if Jack stole the neighbors' hens

My grandmother tried to feed the puppy
what the family grew and ate
Jack ate a little bread but nothing else
Jack was thin and hungry
Saruzzu loved Jack
told his mother he'd teach Jack
to eat *"'na santa cosa"*
that they grew and stored
a miracle of life and energy: the fava bean

One day Saruzzu, his pockets filled with fava beans
walked with Jack through the fields
He chewed a fava bean   offered it to Jack
who sniffed but did not eat

Saruzzu threw favas in the air
caught them in his mouth
chewed and ate them with delight
This was a game Jack wanted to play

Saruzzu tossed a fava high into the air
Jack leaped, caught it in his mouth, ate every bit
over and over each day
Saruzzu and Jack played the game
Soon Jack ate favas even without the game

Jack was full   Jack grew strong
Jack never killed a chicken
My grandmother praised Saruzzu
her smart little boy
for teaching Jack to love fava beans.

* *'na santa cosa* = a holy thing.

The She-Wolf

Listen, you of Italic blood,
scattered throughout the globe
Listen, I am *La Lupa,* your founding mother,
I suckled you on fierce milk
I taught those pups, Romulus and Remus,
    to circle the den
    marking the loop
    noting the earth's orbit

I say: Be brave.   Go forward and
understand the lupercalian loop
We are strong together
encircled in the loop of life

Search your hands
You will see my lesson
All the swirls of the galaxies
    are written on your skin
All the swirls of the galaxies
    are looped on bark, on leaves
    on the carbon of your flesh

Italic blooded, find your destiny
    in the circling of the loop.

THE ROOSTER:
FOR LINA INSANA

"Cicciu" he called me
a diminutive of his own name, Francesco,
we lived in a cave   in North Italy
he fed me
during those dark, confusing days
of the Second World War

I crowed and strutted while he worked
I got used to his Sicilian tongue
though I was a proud *Alt'Italia* rooster

we were males   without women
firelight,   oil lamp
it was dim as he worked
he practiced his craft
making shoes for the partisans
    so they could fight sure-footed
making seals for the partisans
    so they could stamp the discharge and
identification papers
    for all in need

He was an honorable man   creative   energetic

    he left the Italian army in disgust
    over fascism's false promises

a Sicilian man and a Northern rooster
    we kept each other company
    till the partisans won
    the war ended
    the farmer returned and
    I ruled a harem once again

The grape vines told me
Francesco returned to Sicily
then traveled to a faraway land
he took a beautiful bride
fathered beautiful children

I kept the name Cicciu
because I was a proud *Alt'Italia* rooster
who wished to honor Francesco Insana
my human companion
of long ago.

The Elephant

They sold my friend Betty
She screamed for me
when they put the electric prods to her sides
they loaded her into a truck
she cried a sad farewell to me
when they drove her far off from me

They sold my friend   Betty
My heart hurts
I hope it stops

I've forgotten the dance I'm supposed to do
they sold Betty
I've lost my balance
cannot stand on the stool
they sold Betty
I am alone
I cry tears they don't see
my heart hurts
I hope it stops

They use electric prods on me
I can't remember what to do
in the ring
I am a big dummy
they sold Betty
my heart hurts
I hope it stops

Maria Famà   *31*

Here in the circus ring
the laughing, yelling faces
the prods
they sold Betty
I hurt
I see a bit of sunlight
I run towards it
yelling faces under my feet
so easy to crush their skulls
their bones no more than twigs
beneath me

I run
overturn the cars in the lot
I run
across the highway
they sold Betty
my heart hurts
maybe it will stop

I run onto the sidewalk
push through a shop's plate glass window
overturn the tables
taste the bitter pastries on the shelves
no sweetness
no softness
they sold my friend Betty
I must crush everything in my path

They sold Betty
I am alone
a bullet in my side
another   another   another

I am on my knees
my heart hurts
they sold Betty
my heart hurts
it will stop
it will stop

Swimming with the Sharks

I, a small cunning fish,
  cannot swim with the sharks anymore

I admire their sharpness, their quickness
            their intensity
            their beauty and their skill

I, a small smart fish
  once swam with sharks
  played with sharks
  tried to be a shark

Now, I must go far away to hide and heal
I am tired
I cannot swim with the sharks anymore
they will smell my weakness
I am prey
I falter
make false moves
I have a slight wound
the sharks will smell the tiny trickle of my blood
they'll surround and kill

I am a small fish
I must go far from those
I so admire

I am prey

I cannot swim with the sharks anymore.

King of the Rats

In the time of my ancestors
humans built this subway for us
they ride the trains   stand on platforms
think my realm is theirs
but our nests are here
where it is cool and dark
there are juicy wires to gnaw upon
an escalator in which to play
there are no cats here

I am the King of the Rats
I walk along the rails as humans cringe
my power is great
yes, they throw poison, set traps
only a few of us die
we have many young
our coats glisten
we grow strong on the thrown away
human foods and cans of soda and beer

When I stroll with my pack of guards
heading for the escalator
the humans freeze.
I smell their fear.
I, the King of the Rats, can read
their puny minds, their simple feelings
I know they fear our bite
I know the urge sometimes comes upon them
to throw themselves in front of a moving train

I know they fear being thrown onto the tracks
by one of their own
I know they are afraid they will slip, fall,
be dismembered, die on the third rail

As I survey my kingdom
I stride past the sleepy early morning riders
I glide past the shrieking laughing students
I saunter past the weary wary night riders

I am powerful
I am the King of the Rats.

Mzee

I have seen one hundred twenty years
　come and go
　some good　some bad
I carry my grey shell high and light
as all giant tortoises do
slow and deliberate in sun or rain
I walk the paths
　of Mombasa's Haller Park Animal Facility

I am called Mzee
Swahili for old man
yet I have much life in me yet

When the baby hippo approached
I was sunning myself
he had been swept down the Subaki River
　into the Indian Ocean
　when the tsunami hit
torn from his mother's side
only one year old
humans found him on the shore
dehydrated, calling for his mother
they named him Owen
I don't know what that means

humans could not bring him to another hippo herd
no hope for a baby male without a Mamma
older males would kill him

Owen was scared, crying for his Mamma
when they brought him to this sanctuary
he spotted me, so big and grey in the sunshine
lumbered up to me, snuggled against my shell

in my life I have seen so far
one hundred twenty years
come and go
some good   some bad
Owen had only one bad year
he needed a mother and chose me

I am male but my heart is kind
I can calm this baby
  we walk together
  we swim together
  we eat together
  we sleep together

I stretch my long neck and nuzzle
his big round head

I have seen one hundred twenty years
come and go
some good   some bad
this year is good for Owen and me

MARIA FAMÀ   *39*

the humans hope that in five years
Owen will make friends with
a young female hippo here in the sanctuary

but for now

I, Mzee, an old giant tortoise
will mother Owen, the baby hippo.

Skeeter (1987–2008)

She was Skeeter, Skeetie, Puss-Cake, Puddy-Cat,
         Girlfriend, Skeets, and My Little Girl
She was my feline companion for 21 years

I knew about Skeeter before she was born
Her mother was the J&A Caterers cat
  famous for her beautiful babies
my brother who worked there asked if I wanted
one of the kittens   I said yes
Skeeter came to live with me
as soon as she was weaned at six weeks old
the first day of her life with me
she mewed for her mother   I was there
over the next 21 years of her life
Skeeter gained six pounds
She was lithe and feisty   petite and cautious
Skeeter was Zen in her calming spirit
                  Operatic in her loud vocalizations
                  beatific in her purrings

My father, a professional artist
painted Skeeter's portrait in oil
sculpted Skeeter's likeness in marble
he was fascinated by
                  her classic tabby forehead
                  her heart shaped face
                  her knowing green eyes
he was enchanted by
                  her black, beige, gray, brown

striped fur
her supple, agile body
her demure way of sitting
with her tail curled around herself

Skeeter got phone calls
Skeeter got fan mail
humans seemed drawn to her
other animals gave her respect

Skeeter scanned her territory with care:
a walk in the morning with me
out the front door up Sigel Street towards Passyunk
Avenue
intrepid as other cats watched from windows
birds surrounded us on wires, trees, and fences
dogs and humans passed us by
later Skeeter checked the backyard, cellar, first and
second floor
she observed the neighborhood
  from the front picture window
  from the backyard rose tree

Skeeter was attentive to the phone:
running to stand beside it when it rang
the call might have been for her
since my friends called her to say "hello"
when I was not at home
they left messages for her on the answering machine
as I did when I called her from work
I wanted Skeeter to hear my voice

Skeeter was attentive to the mail:
when the mailman approached our house
Skeeter walked to the door   sat by the mail slot
as envelopes fell to the floor
she sniffed each one before
walking away satisfied

Living so many years with me, a writer,
Skeeter loved books, papers, magazines
she chewed on my pens and notebooks
walked on the computer keyboard
pulled books off the shelves
whenever I read the newspaper
Skeeter made sure to sit on it
sniffing all the news
from abroad   from the USA
she smelled all the photos
                    of disasters
                    of sales
                    of crying people
                    of smiling politicians

Skeeter was well informed on faraway places
she scrutinized all bags and shoes
that entered our home
rubbing her return messages to those other places
filled with their cats, people, dogs, ferrets, birds,
                    fish, and other creatures

Skeeter oversaw all the students I tutored
She'd sit on the table

watching them as
they struggled over their lessons
she viewed them with concern
she let them pet her for encouragement
she calmed their anxieties

My Skeeter was a rescue cat
many times she warned me of danger
waking me with loud meows and taps to my nose
until I roused to follow her
to wherever she led me:
the flooded basement   the broken water heater
burning pots and fiery pans
rain-soaked kitchen   damaged bathroom ceiling

Skeeter sometimes caught mice and birds
leaving them untouched for me
to admire her loving gifts
to praise her hunting prowess

Skeeter enjoyed her food
She ate cat food, relished treats and catnip,
she prized biscotti and pizzelle
provided they were made with anise oil
she loved broccoli rabe, peas, carrots
sweet potatoes, spinach, birthday cake,
grated pecorino cheese, soy ice cream,
ham and turkey alternating every week
from the grocer who knew her tastes
two weeks before she passed
Skeeter made a flying leap onto the dining room table
to eat most of a vegetarian burrito

which I'd planned on eating myself

Skeeter was fond of drinking hot water
  from the bathtub faucet
she learned as a kitten to jump in the tub
jiggle the old faucet until she got a nice, hot drip
a kind of tea
she drank until she passed into eternal life

Skeeter was with me through
painful times of sickness and loss
and joyful times of triumph and festivities
her presence always soothing and patient

Skeeter made sure we had our love sessions
at least twice a day
Each morning was intense petting time
After her walk   after she was fed
I ate my breakfast and stroked her
as she sat by me and purred
every evening was snuggle petting time on the sofa
she'd groom me by licking my hair
before settling down on or beside me
to watch TV or listen to music on CD

On the day before she died
Skeeter mewed like a kitten
while walking through the house.
I petted her, cuddled her, spoke to her
but I sensed she was calling to her mother
              she was returning to her mother

MARIA FAMÀ   45

Skeeter died peacefully in the morning
giving me one parting meow of farewell

Each day with Skeeter was full
                                was rich
                                was lively

I was blessed by her presence in my life

I am grateful that we had

a long and loving relationship.

Feral Cats

My Roman friend Pino
tells me all the cats of Rome
are ancient Romans
returned to live in
the ruins of the beloved forums
theaters and temples
they built as humans long ago

The cats wander the alleys
and cobbled streets
at five in the afternoon
they sit on ancient walls
and tumbled columns
at various ruined sites
waiting for their ladies
the *gattaie*
in their flowered dresses
and backless shoes
who bring the cats pasta
in aluminum foil.

The feral cats know it is their due
a small, fitting tribute
to them, the ancients
who built the eternal city.

Work

I head to work
leave Dolly my caped tabby cat home
lounging on the sofa
food and water at the ready
Dolly has lined up my shoes upstairs
outside my bedroom door
later she'll bring them downstairs
to make designs and constructions
while I'm away

A block from the high rise where I work
I pass a bearded young beggar
sitting under a tree
an orange cat
a leash around his neck
sits upright and poised on the beggar's lap
no food or water in sight
the cat attracts attention and money

I cross busy Market Street to my job
I tutor   I teach
food and water in my backpack
cat or human
we work at tasks heavy or light
we all do what we must.

Gulls

Neptune is in my first house
so in my head
I'M TALL

I stand at the green flecked water's edge
long to bolt
umbrella shadows

I long to embrace the vastness

The rebel yells of gulls
entice me
I watch

                        the seagulls
                                tumbling
                                through
                                sky shafts

The gulls call me

to kiss like them
the restless cheeks of foam

Neptune is in my first house
so in my head
I'M STRONG

Maria Famà   *49*

I yearn to embrace the vastness

The gulls laugh

dive and rise

I cannot escape
with them

    into the mist-formed clouds

I am short, wingless, fragile
I can only embrace the vastness

from the shore

Seagull

I awoke to a seagull's call
  on this morning of menstrual blood
  in a morning when the city air
contained clouds and melting snow

Sixty miles from the ocean
my bed is a ship
tossed with pain and dreams
  yet on this day
I arose different, refreshed

A seabird flew through the fog
  over my house
  called me a blessing

the search for sustenance
  was joyous
the ocean's expanse
  within reach.

Bird in the Fig Tree

The gray feathered bird sits in a September fig tree
next to a window in a Philadelphia backyard
he whistles, chirps, and warbles
singing his own songs
in time to Neapolitan music I play on cassette

Santa Lucia Lontana

> How far are we really, little friend,
> from the Mediterranean shore?

I' te vurría vasá

> Sure voiced creature, how many kisses
> can you earn with a song?

Tu ca nun chiagne

> Do you cry for those not with you?
> Do others long for you?

Gray feathered one, you feast on the season's last figs
between songs as I change the tape

Piscatore 'e Pusilleco

> Your wings lift you to where
> there is sun and sea

the fig tree will be covered soon
the snow will come
you will sing with full heart
in another part of the world.

How to Talk

"Play this record everyday three times a day"
the *Teach Your Parakeet To Talk* booklet said
   the summer I was nine
"If you follow these directions carefully
 your parakeet will talk within a month"

Chico could whistle tunes
sit on my finger
kiss my nose
climb toy ladders
but I wanted him to talk
      Everyday in the steamy July kitchen
      from ten to eleven
          two to three
          four to five
    I played the record
    Amid chirps and squawks, real parakeets said
words
    after a lady said them first
    "Sweetheart! Sweetheart!"
    "I love you. I love you."
    "Hello, baby, want a kiss?"

    Everyday my baby brother crawled in diapers
    to sit by the record player
    Chico cocked his green head
    black eyes attentive
    as I spun the disk for weeks

my baby brother repeated after the lady
and repeated after the birds
"Hello, baby, want a kiss?"
"Need a cracker now!"
"I love you, sweetheart."
Chico whistled his appreciation
when the record lady spoke
when the record birds spoke
when my brother spoke

Chico never learned to speak
I did not ask for my money back
the record did teach a baby to talk
within a month.

Spike and Lou

As if protecting the whole world
six legs came down the street on a cool morning
Spike and Lou side by side
a dog and a man
sturdy and robust
fur and hair neat and brushed
side by side, resolute, brave
Spike and Lou came down the street on a cool
morning
it is easy to believe
in safety   in well being
when stalwart Spike and hearty Lou
walk in the world on a cool morning.

STORM

Remember when I used to lie
flat on my back and watch the ceiling
from the middle of the floor?
I liked to pretend I was walking
in an upside-down world of
floating stairs and high-up doors.

Remember how surprised I was when
Midnight, the cat, sat on my stomach
while I was ceiling walking?
You said the cat was pretending
I was his sofa
and I began to laugh and
Midnight, sitting straight, stared at me
as he rose and fell with
each spasm of hilarity
I hooted but Midnight kept as still
and steady as a Captain on a sea-tossed
gale blown ship
gazing evenly at me
the cause of this storm.

I shrieked, tears rained hard
I hurt, and gasped for breath
Finally, when I was still,
silent, exhausted
the cat stepped carefully down
and followed you
out the door.

PET

A turtle was delivered
   special delivery from Louisiana

I had filled out the order form from
the back of a comic book and sent the money
I had saved for this pet

Alone, he traveled through the mail
in a small box with tiny holes
and was delivered, scratching the cardboard,
   to our city door

Turtle, did you wish for heavy, humid air
   the slowness of swamps
   the taste of fresh caught flies?

We placed you in a plastic bowl
   sprinkled colored pebbles in your path
   tossed in some processed bugs from the pet store

The room was air conditioned
outside the air was hot and damp

Turtle, I secretly longed to set you free
   but where would you go
   along the city's streets?

You were now my pet.

Mad Dog

The cops are afraid
    to leave their sky blue cars

The guns bulge black and stupid
    at their sides

All the orders of the Law
    are paralyzed
    by one crazed dog
    who foams and growls
    from a shattered window

No one is home

The curtains flare out into the winds
    struggling
    with the savage cold
    scolding the animal sweat
    that mired
    their pristine elegance

The barks warn of enemies

The neighbors were alarmed

No one is home

Who will interpret for the dog his fears?

Officers, sirens, schoolchildren?

Only the curtains
trapped and mute

plead the case

for icy winds and

mad dog.

FOR GREGORY B.

According to Gregory Bateson, epistemologist,
        as quoted in *The Tarrytown Newsletter,*
poets must allow stones and animals to speak.
"We must listen to voices other than our own."

Gregory, in January,
at my approach
Allegheny Avenue pigeons eating a dropped
hamburger and bun
mouths too full to speak
shot me mustard-yellow snow-iced evil eyes

I bent over
a leftover brown, brittle leaf that quaked
on the Walnut Street Subway steps
it shrugged and blew toward Locust Street

The stones around City Hall Courtyard
are stoical but too tired to talk
rain and piss wear them down and
the concrete, being man-made,
is both cracked and articulate
"Fuck off," I was told

My mother's cat, Prim, sitting by the refrigerator,
let me know
she liked breaded chicken cutlets better than fresh
    sparrows

she favors *merluzzo in bianco* rather than Tender
    Vittles

Paulie's dog, Lady, outside the grooming center
cursed the bows in her fur
Poodles are oppressed
pink boots make her paws sweat

Gregory,
self-satisfied, urbane roaches
send to poets, pirates, pawns, and kings a message
"Order more pizza and Chinese food
ban all roach motels
stop the senseless war against us
escalation of weapons is pointless
we will survive nuclear blast
coexistence is the only way."

Duet

Early in the morning
  on a small street
early in the morning
  on a Tuesday
a lady sat angry on her front steps
  hollering at her dog
"You bother me early in the morning!
Early in the morning!"

Early in the morning
  on a small street
early in the morning
  on a Tuesday
a big, glossy black, female dog stood
  howling at her lady,
  in a plaintive, canine voice
  came the approximate sound
"Early in the morning!
Early in the morning!"

Early in the morning
  as the sun was rising
early in the morning
  on a small street
early in the morning
  on a Tuesday
an angry woman kept repeating
  "Early in the morning! Early in the morning!"

Maria Famà   *63*

Her dog sang right along
"Early in the morning! Early in the morning!"

Cleaning Fish

The white fish is rife with bones

I separate
prong-like scales
ready to stab
ready to choke

Off with the shocked head.

Do horses eat fish when they can't get hay?

I dreamt of a little white horse
A fish skeleton of troubles sat on my plate
The dream horse pranced on the table,
ate fish flesh from my hand.

The tiny dream horse is either
        you or Pegasus

Pegasus may have come, stunning, shining
to bestow magic and grace

Fish as poetry

Or it was you, eating from my hand.

Sweet and docile as I can never have you

Or could it be that you devour
my Pisces fish sign sun-self

Picking me clean,
leaving the bones
I fastidiously remove

The head long gone. The heart eaten.

Committee Haiku

The committee sits
papers and deep discussion
sparrows on the sill.

Pigeon

It's true
I really saw
a pigeon at Temple University
land wing-deep in snow
on the back lawn of the Student Union Building

It's true
I really saw
how the pigeon walked in huge arcs
making designs in untouched white

It's true
I really saw
the pigeon fly off
leaving in the snow
two joined outlines
one of a horse
one of a pigeon

It's true
I really saw.

For the Birds

My grandmother delighted
in throwing into her large backyard
  cereal, fruit, lunchmeat, pasta, bread
  every leftover from every meal
  for the birds

My grandmother almost starved in Sicily
during the Second World War
  without any bread
  she lived on some olives   some fruit
  whatever she managed to grow and save

In her New Jersey home
she cooked fresh for herself and my grandfather
  when they finished
  she tossed with abandon
  veal cutlets, salad, sausages, string beans,
  meatballs, macaroni, greens, soup
  into her yard
  for the birds

It was a thrill tinged with bitterness
she had so much now
  she never had to eat a leftover

Only when we visited from Philadelphia
did my grandmother refrain from throwing out
  most of the Sunday or holiday dinner
  because my mother asked her for the leftovers

to make our lunches for the next day

My mother reasoned that surely
we could eat as well as those birds
  of every type
  who flocked to my grandmother's yard from miles
around

My grandmother was not starving
we were not starving
  neither were the birds.

Not Killing:
For Anita

We chased flies out the door with dish towels
we tiptoed around spider webs, sweeping ants
    into the yard
She was upset that her nephew squashed a spider
    with delight
yet she killed herself demurely, cleanly
if a spider deserved to live, so did she.

Ebony and Ivory

Ebony and Ivory, two year old pigs
in a Penn State study,
were taught computer games

Ebony and Ivory pushed a joystick with their mouths
the ultimate goal, the scientists said,
was to teach the pigs to communicate with humans

The scientists said
"if farmers knew what pigs wanted
they could breed them better
they could make more money"

Ebony and Ivory learned the icons
for hungry   for thirsty
for cold   for hot
they learned choices of food and drink

Ebony and Ivory and their kin
destined to be eaten as hams, sausages, and chops
made into footballs and purses,
will not learn computer icons for
"we are imprisoned"
"you have killed our mother"
"you exploit"   "you butcher"

Ebony and Ivory did not learn to say

"you cannot hear us"

"you do not know us."

Dolly, the Cloned Sheep

Dolly, the first cloned sheep
   raised as an experiment in a barnyard lab
   is dead

Dolly quickly aged as soon as she was born

When my father was a small boy
learning to tend sheep
in the mountain fields of Sicily
he said to his mother that all the sheep sounded alike

Baaa Baaa Baaa Baaa
was all they said

"How can a lamb find his mother?" he asked

My grandmother answered,
"Don't you recognize my voice
when I call you in a crowd?
The lamb knows his mother's own voice."

Spirit of Dolly, cloned, quickly aged and dead,
your lambdom was over before it began
your body soon older than the ewe who nursed you

Dolly, arthritic, infirm, young, cloned sheep,
did you and all the cloned animals
all aging and dying so fast

ever somehow someway
get a bit of mother love?

August Rush Hour

Crickets sing in the summer subway station

at seven thirty in the morning

temperature in the nineties

high humidity

Crickets sing in the subway

as if it were

a starbright summer evening.

CRICKET

A cricket sings in my kitchen
snug behind the stove
he plays his forewings
while outside, cool autumn winds blow

Cricket in the kitchen
ancient Chinese emperors would prize you
put you in a gilded box
to sing them to sleep
I, instead, appreciate you
there behind the stove
with a song that brings me joy
as I cook, eat, wash dishes

When I sweep the floor
I leave a few crumbs for you
cricket in the kitchen, behind the stove,
thank you.

Whale Watch

You and I on the rolling deck of the old ship
eating breadsticks so we wouldn't get seasick
bundled up in August on the Atlantic,
staring at the horizon
we waited for the whales

Hand in hand we ran
from port to starboard
and back to port
waiting for the whales
who come to Provincetown
with dolphin friends

Dolphins laughed and swam silvery
near the boat
I leaned over the rail
touched a dolphin's back
thrilled beyond measure
You laughed and kissed me quick
then someone shouted, "Whales!"

Little and awed we stood close on the deck
and watched a breach:
bluish gray   gorgeous
huge as a bus
a whale launched high into the air
and back into the deep

We cheered, jumped up and down, hugged
we were so tiny, so humbled, so exalted
to see a living giant
  carefree in the waves
  beautiful as the ocean
            as the earth
            as love
            as home.

Acknowledgements

GRATEFUL ACKNOWLEDGMENT is made to the editors of the following publications, in which some of the poems in this book first appeared: *Bel Tesoro Press Broadside, Breaking Open, La Bella Figura, Laurel Leaves, Liberty Hill Poetry Review, Mad Poets Review, Modern Haiku, Paterson Literary Review, Philadelphia Poets, Sisters Singing.*

THE FOLLOWING POEMS were previously published in: *Philadelphia Poets:* "Work" (2016), "Nelle" (2014), "Skeeter" (2010), "Mzee" and "Elephant" (2006), "Cricket" (2004), "The Lion" and "The King of the Rats" (2003). *Mia Mamma* anthology (2006, Winston Publishing, Pittsford, NY): "For the Birds." *Sisters Singing: Incantations, Blessings, Chants, Prayers, and Sacred Stories from Women Writers* (2006, Wild Girl Publishing, Santa Cruz, CA): "Canyon de Chelly" (first published in *Liberty Hill Poetry Review,* 1995). *Paterson Literary Review* (2004): "Not Killing." *Breaking Open: Reflections on Italian American Women's Writing* (2003, Purdue University Press, West Lafayette, IN): "The Rooster." *Mad Poets Review* (2000): "Horses." *Hey!* (1998): "August Rush Hour" and "Storm." *Schuykill Valley Journal* (1994 Dream Images issue): "Cleaning Fish." *La Bella Figura: A Choice anthology* (1994, Malafemmina Press, San Francisco, CA): "Feral Cats." *Bel Tesoro Press Broadside* (1992, Philadelphia, PA): "She-Wolf." *Modern Haiku* (1998): "Committee Haiku."

About the Author

ARIA FAMÀ IS THE AUTHOR of six books of po-
etry. Her work appears in numerous publications
and anthologies. She was a finalist and two-time
Editor's Choice winner in the Allen Ginsberg Poetry
Awards.

Famà has read her poetry in many cities across the
country, read one of her stories on National Public
Radio, co-founded a video production company, and
recorded her poetry for CD compilations of music
and poetry. She appears reading her poems in the films
Prisoners Among Us, Pipes of Peace, and *La Mia Strada.*

Famà's poems were awarded the 2002 and 2005
Aniello Lauri Award in Creative Writing. In 2006 she
won the Amy Tritsch Needle Award for Poetry. Her
recent books *Looking For Cover* (2008) and *Mystics in
the Family* (2013) were published by Bordighera Press.

Maria Famà lives and works in Philadelphia, PA.

About Pearlsong Press

Pearlsong Press is an independent publishing company
dedicated to providing books and resources that entertain
while expanding perspectives on the self and the world. The
company was founded by Peggy Elam, Ph.D., a psychologist and
journalist, in 2003.

We encourage you to enjoy other Pearlsong Press books, which
you can purchase at www.pearlsong.com or your favorite bookstore.
Keep up with us through our blog at www.pearlsongpress.com as
we promote health and happiness at every size.

Fiction

Heretics: A Love Story & *The Singing of Swans*
novels about the divine feminine by Mary Saracino
Judith—an historical novel by Leslie Moïse
Fatropolis—a paranormal adventure by Tracey L. Thompson
*The Falstaff Vampire Files, Bride of the Living Dead, Larger Than
Death, Large Target, At Large* & *A Ton of Trouble*
paranormal adventure, romantic comedy
& Josephine Fuller mysteries by Lynne Murray
The Season of Lost Children—a novel by Karen Blomain
Fallen Embers & *Blowing Embers*—Books 1 & 2 of
The Embers Series, paranormal romance by Lauri J Owen
The Program & *The Fat Lady Sings*
suspense & young adult novels by Charlie Lovett
Syd Arthur—a novel by Ellen Frankel
Measure By Measure—a romantic romp with the fabulously fat
by Rebecca Fox & William Sherman
FatLand & *FatLand: The Early Days*
Books 1 & 2 of The FatLand Trilogy by Frannie Zellman

Romance Novels & Short Stories Featuring Big Beautiful Heroines

by Pat Ballard, the Queen of Rubenesque Romances:
Once Upon Another Time | *Adam & Evelyn* | *ASAP Nanny* |
Dangerous Love | *The Best Man* | *Abigail's Revenge* | *Dangerous*

Curves Ahead: Short Stories | Wanted: One Groom | Nobody's Perfect
| His Brother's Child | A Worthy Heir
by Rebecca Brock—*The Giving Season*
& by Judy Bagshaw—*Kiss Me, Nate!* & *At Long Last, Love*

Nonfiction
Soul Mothers' Wisdom: Seven Insights for the Single Mother
by Bette J. Freedson
Acceptable Prejudice? Fat, Rhetoric & Social Justice & *Talking Fat:*
Health vs. Persuasion in the War on Our Bodies
by Lonie McMichael, Ph.D.
Hiking the Pack Line: Moving from Grief to a Joyful Life
by Bonnie Shapbell
A Life Interrupted: Living with Brain Injury
poetry by Louise Mathewson
ExtraOrdinary: An End of Life Story Without End
memoir by Michele Tamaren & Michael Wittner
Love is the Thread: A Knitting Friendship by Leslie Moïse, Ph.D.
Fat Poets Speak: Voices of the Fat Poets' Society & *Fat Poets Speak 2:*
Living and Loving Fatly—Frannie Zellman, Ed.
10 Steps to Loving Your Body (No Matter What Size You Are)
by Pat Ballard
Something to Think About: Reflections on Life, Family, Body Image
& Other Weighty Matters by the Queen of Rubenesque Romances
by Pat Ballard
Beyond Measure: A Memoir About Short Stature & Inner Growth
by Ellen Frankel
Taking Up Space: How Eating Well & Exercising Regularly Changed
My Life by Pattie Thomas, Ph.D. with Carl Wilkerson, M.B.A.
(foreword by Paul Campos, author of *The Obesity Myth*)
Off Kilter: A Woman's Journey to Peace with Scoliosis, Her Mother
& Her Polish Heritage—a memoir by Linda C. Wisniewski
Unconventional Means: The Dream Down Under
a spiritual travelogue by Anne Richardson Williams
Splendid Seniors: Great Lives, Great Deeds
inspirational biographies by Jack Adler

HEALING THE WORLD ONE BOOK AT A TIME